THE COMPLETE GUIDE TO JAPANESE
KIMONO FABRICS: From Silk to Shibori,
Mastering the Craft

Keith Jared

Table of Contents

CHAPTER ONE

INTRODUCTION

The Japanese kimono surface is worldwide outstanding as a wonderful and flabbergasting eco-obliging elective surface to plastic shopping sacks, covers, and so forth. These things are consistently created utilizing cotton, silk, nylon, or rayon and are known as a Furoshiki. It could additionally have standard Japanese models like family apexes or kimono plans with gathering of arrangements. Kyoto has spots where they utilize the standard specialty of passing on and finishing the Japanese kimono surface and add subtleties to it. Various a shockingly lengthy time span back, this surface was utilized for specific reasons a ton of like today. In any case, from the get go, the furoshiki used to be an immense sheet used to wrap and store clothing while simultaneously visiting a shower house. Properly, "Furo" suggests shower in Japanese. In any case, the material turned out to be some unique choice from that. It was along these lines used to wrap delicate things.

Today, the eminent materials are right now utilized today, frequently as a gift-wrap that, in itself changes into an evergreen gift. A piece of the time, the gift-wrap is more regarded than the certifiable gift and it isn't seen as an impoliteness to re-gift the gift-wrap.

The genuine material is arranged so it will overall be tied really with the utilization of groups in making packs, gift wrapped things, skirts, summer tops or even covers and essentially regardless a particular tendencies. Many pushed stand-apart locaters of the furoshiki use it as upgrades at home or make it utilitarian like for use in enhancing liners. It will overall be utilized regular or during occasions.

Wrap up anything with this sort of material and make it more delightful than its genuine substance. Sizes can sway from fairly square to a long square shape, yet it relies heavily on how you use it and what to wrap will be.

The use includes basically of a major series of groups that are essentially to get the furoshiki. Say for instance, begin taking two opposite sides and tie it just. Take the other two corners and tie it in like manner.

This is the most immediate methodology to wrap gifts or convey things and limits as an unprejudiced satchel as well! There are different styles of packs that can be utilized to make sacks. It very well may be loads with long and short handles or sacks with bamboo ring handles. These particular surfaces can be changed into boleros, summer wear tops, or boleros. You can wrap gifts too with this totally versatile and new look! You'll leave your companion contemplating what's inside that beguiling pack persistently with your furoshiki conveyed using Japanese kimono surface.

THE JAPANESE KIMONO AND THE ESSENTIALS OF THIS STANDARD JAPANESE CLOTHING

The Japanese kimono should be visible as today as one of the world's for the most part flawless and excessive standard dress, and its brilliance comes not just from the stunning tones and parts of its plan, which stresses its wearer's tendency for class and unassumingness, yet likewise in the cautious way by which every one of them is made, which mirror its expert's eye for significance and predominance in making a remarkable Asian dress that can rise above both time and culture.

THE KIMONO ALL THROUGH THE ENTIRE PRESENCE OF JAPAN

All through the entire presence of Japan, the term kimono at first suggested "something to wear" and before the T-molded, lower leg length robe, with covering end on the front, which we know today, was considered as the customary Japanese apparel, the kimono as the standard Japanese dress genuinely went through different changes concerning style, surface, and plan from being chamber framed clothing with openings for the sleeves that were worn by the

Japanese ranchers on the fields to the kimono which were styled after the Chinese cheongsam and pants (for men) and skirts (for ladies) which, at a certain point, were worn with Korean-styled coats, and eventually the rich, lower leg length, and wrinkle over robes that were gotten at the midriff together with an obi.

Japanese Kimono's Game plan

The normal Japanese dress or kimono is a lower leg length, T-formed outfit with wide and long streaming sleeves and covering style front end plan. It is then added at the midriff with an obi, which assists with keeping it imploded over the body.

Such Kimono Surface

Standard Japanese kimono surfaces, similar to the Nishijin-ori, Chirimen or crepe, Kinran (gold brocade), and Ginran (silver brocade), which are woven from standard silk strings, are utilized to make the Japanese kimonos. In any case, considering the at present excessive expense to make and finish kimonos that are made using these standard Japanese kimono surfaces, brief or current decisions rather than something practically indistinguishable, similar to silk, rayon, wool, brocade, jacquard, polyester, and cotton, or a mix of something practically indistinguishable, are utilized to and they are then obvious by hands or utilizing a machine to copy the energy of customary

Japanese kimono surfaces. Silk kimonos stay a model 1, particularly for surprising events, while polyester kimonos are regularly regarded for how they duplicate the energy of silk kimonos for a piece of the last decision's expense, and cotton or fleece are continually respected for decent kimono dressing.

CHAPTER TWO

KIMONO SLEEVES

Wide and long, streaming sleeves see a Japanese kimono from other kimono-style clothing. Since the past periods, kimono robes with extra-long, influencing sleeves, which length could appear at up to the knees, are held for the lady, while those with extra confined sleeves, or which could appear at up to the waist, are worn by the wedded ladies. For the easygoing kimono robes or summer robes, called the yukata, the disconnecting component in the sleeves essentially comes in whether it is worn by a man or lady with men's yukata having more limited, streaming sleeves when stood apart from the ladies' yukata.

Kimono's Obi Belt

Japanese kimonos' obi belt, all over, measure twelve (12) inches wide, and they can be made utilizing something basically the equivalent or another perpetually shade of surface as the kimono. A little pad is generally gotten at the rear of a female kimono wearer to keep her obi belt and kimono got, or the obi might be tied in an illuminating way, as appearing to be a bow or butterfly, so they go probably as a superb detail to the rear of the kimono robe.

KIMONO SUBTLETIES AND PLANS

A Japanese kimono's stunning game plan might be painted, grouping tinted, or twisted onto their surface, or such might be made by surprisingly concealing the silk strings that will be utilized to make them and carefully turning around something practically indistinguishable from make a kimono robe with the trained professional's or their wearer's ideal model.

Figures and photographs of the Japanese cherry fledgling, chrysanthemum, lotus, peony, phoenix, pre-winter leaves, and the Japanese geisha, are famous subjects of the Japanese kimono robes for ladies, while prints of the dragonfly, winged snake, and the kanzi making, as well as wavy, striped, or repeated strong block figures are commonplace among the Japanese kimono for men.

Kimono Size

Japanese kimonos, overall, can be worn across a few size ranges inferable from the free game plan, so you won't anytime need to stress creating of your kimono with the development of time.

What proportion of time does it Hope to Make a Japanese Kimono?

Kimono robes should be possible for as short as inside the day or for something like six (6) months, subject to the straightforwardness or diverse nature of their course of action, the limit of their producer, and the accessibility of the surfaces that are utilized to make them.

HOW TO SAVE WHILE SHOPPING A JAPANESE KIMONO

It is normal to find an extremely fine and wonderful kimono robes today that expense as much as a shining clean vehicle, notwithstanding, you can in any case save while a shopping am certified Japanese kimono by purchasing model or utilized kimonos; old yet great kimono textures, which come from old kimono texture rolls or acquired from destroyed kimonos; or, you can shop the slow time of year assortments or dead loads of the Japanese kimono makers, Japanese kimono shop, or Asian stores around the world.

THE ADVANCEMENT OF THE PLAN OF THE JAPANESE KIMONO

We should step into the beautiful universe of the Japanese kimono robes with a concise history of the development of its plan through the ages.

Which began as a Japanese kimono?

In the days of yore, the Japanese expression, kimono, in a real sense makes an interpretation of to 'something to wear' and envelop the various sorts of dress that were ordinarily worn by the Japanese, yet presently.

The Jomon Time frame Kimono

With the hunting and assembling way of life of the Japanese during the time, the customary Japanese dress was said to have been made of fur and was hung freely around the body.

Yayoi Period Kimono

With the presentation of rice farming, the Japanese kimono was supposed to be a free piece of clothing with openings to put the arms through and which empowered their wearer to be agreeable while dealing with the rice fields. The geta, or wooden shoes, which are generally matched today with the easygoing Japanese Yukata, was supposed to be created.

Kofun Period Kimono

The main silk kimono was made during this time and the kimono style was propelled by the Chinese and Korean robes, which were shut to the front and tied at the midriff without buttons and had skirts or pants, which were frequently finished with a brilliantly hued robe.

Asuka Period Kimono

With the advancement of the sewing techniques, the Kofun-time frame coat or kimono robe was made longer and with more extensive sleeves. During this time, the retainers' garments were likewise partitioned into three (3), i.e., formal garments, court garments which was duplicated from the Chinese court dress, and outfits.

Nara Period Kimono

The early Nara Time frame Yoro Code expected that all kimono robes be gotten left over right, similar to the Chinese, which turned into the show of how the Japanese kimono robe is wrapped until now. The method involved with coloring the kimono was additionally evolved during this period and the essential kimono was for the most part made of one tone. The kimono likewise turned into a superficial point of interest in that the respectable men wore a free upper piece of clothing with a cut on the two sides, the ladies wore a short upper piece of clothing and a long, streaming skirt, with the court individuals wearing them in colors that imply their position. The ordinary citizens, then again, dressed a lot more straightforward, i.e., the men wore pants over kimono-like upper pieces of clothing with tight sleeves and band and ladies wore a kimono-like upper article of clothing which covered right to left and that is worn over short underwear and a skirt.

Heian Period Kimono:

Straight-cut kimono-production method was created, which made it simpler for the Japanese to make kimono out of a wide range of kinds of texture, wear them in layers throughout the colder time of year, and utilizing a light texture during summer. Further improvement of kimono-coloring techniques likewise made ready for beautiful, apparently creatively worked kimonos and wearing season-explicit kimono tones was viewed as a standard.

Edo Period Kimono

Yet again oppose coloring, or Yuzen coloring, created during this period, subsequently the kimono had more bright and imaginative materials and became single-layered. The sleeves of the kimono were made longer, particularly among unmarried ladies, the obi scarf was made more extensive, and a few methods of tying the last option became stylish. The kimono likewise turned into a sign of economic wellbeing and the utilization of stifled shaded kimonos additionally became normal.

Meiji Period Kimono

As of now, the kimono was instituted as the T-molded Japanese attire. A few individuals from the first class, particularly the men, began to wear Western-style clothing, similar to matching suits for work, and wear the kimono just at home. Today, the Japanese kimono can be viewed as one of the world's most fortune commendable customary apparel on the planet, not just in light of the typically costly necessary expense to make one, but since of the rich history and culture of Japan that is sewed inside every one of them. Be one of the glad proprietors of a Japanese kimono robe now and see with your own eyes how this valuable Japanese dress can undoubtedly draw out the elegance and style of each and every lady.

CHAPTER THREE

DESIGNS ON THE JAPANESE KIMONO DRESS

With regards to apparel it in every case some way or another mirrors the time and state of mind and even feelings of the wearer and the fashioner. For this reason there are occasional garments that not just have the best occasional textures and materials however they additionally have the right tones and plans for the particular seasons. Garments are a statement of what our identity is and it is a portrayal of what our preferences are. Occasional puts on something else similarly as much as close to home inclinations. Sometime you may be feeling splendid and radiant and would wish to wear something colorful while different times you may be searching for something all the more plain. This is exactly the same thing with the astonishing Japanese kimono dress plans.

Since so many kimono style dress plans are truly in nowadays and numerous originators have planned a few astonishing outfits in that impact, it is smart to become familiar with a smidgen more about kimono dresses and see what the very designs on the Japanese kimonos address. With regards to designs in the kimono, they are basically subject to the occasional changes. They are planned such that the plan mirrors the various seasons and the dress really praises it. Splendid promotion dynamic tones for the spring alongside a few botanical examples are the impression of the warm and radiant climate. The fall plans then again are totally unique and have those ordinary harvest time colors like reddish brown. For winter they have plans including pine trees, bamboo and plum blooms which are known to get karma the colder time of year season and mirror the chilly climate. That's what the Japanese culture directs assuming garments are worn by season they will bring best of luck and heaps of flourishing to the wearer. For this reason they make it a highlight keep the spring garments prepared when winter is disappearing and afterward keep the fall garments helpful when the season starts to show change.

Designs in the kimono plans likewise change because of the degree of custom of a specific occasion. Some plan highlights address lesser convention and others reflect extremely formal clothing. For the most part it is the woven examples and colored tedious examples that are intended for the casual and relaxed occasions and for regular use. For something more conventional which is worn at extraordinary events, the plan become all the more free-form and are available along the stitch or even on the whole kimono surface. Generally numerous layers of kimono clothing were worn which made an impact of variety and dynamic quality and at times they would try and wear up to twelve kimonos in various tones! Albeit that would give the layering impact, inevitably it became regular to straightforward wear the kimono alongside underwear of sorts known as the juban which resembles a slip worn inside the genuine kimono. One more piece of the kimono design is the differing length of the sleeves for ladies that indicate whether a lady is unmarried or hitched. Unmarried ladies wear kimonos with sleeves that are significantly longer.

JAPANESE COTTON TEXTURE IDEAL TEXTURE FOR YOUNGSTERS

Japanese cotton texture is the most well known texture for youngsters and particularly to make wraparounds or wraparound slings to convey children. Albeit numerous different textures like silk, material, fleece are there however the Japanese cotton is the most favored decision. You can purchase natural cotton, with botanical and leaves design, creature, dabs, stripes, twirls, weaves, themes and any remaining examples. This is additionally called kimono that is extremely beautiful and loaded with flower plans.

Benefits

It is an exceptionally delicate and lightweight.

Entirely breathable so you won't feel warmth of summer and coldness of winters.

Because of breathable nature, it gets the water fumes far from the body. On account of this it gives us solace.

As a result of its normally tangled nature it traps the air so give warm protection.

Japanese cotton texture like some other cotton is liberated from any sort of static charge in light of its dampness retaining limit.

Additionally it is hypoallergenic texture, and that implies that it won't make sensitivity the wearers.

This can likewise be treated with UV hindering specialists so will give you phenomenal sun security.

Japanese cotton albeit used to make youngster's material yet the fantastic fire safe property in the wake of treating it prompts its utilization in numerous tactical applications and kids' sleepwear.

This texture is additionally treated with antimicrobial completions.

THE DISTINCTIONS BETWEEN CONVENTIONAL JAPANESE KIMONOS AND KIMONO STYLE DRESSES

Kimono style dresses have acquired prominence in the western world conceivably because of the interest westerners have on Japanese culture. Westerners are most captivated by the way of life of Geishas and with this come the interest with their clothing. These dresses are motivated by conventional Japanese kimonos however don't have the customary obi. They are likewise normally made of a lighter texture, and are typically more limited. These kinds of dresses get the Slipover cut and long sleeves. Notwithstanding, for wear ability purposes, the greater part of them have been abbreviated to the 3/4-a safe distance. They likewise typically integrate the different framing seen on certain kimonos, where the material contrasts on the closures of the arms, the midsection, and the neck area. Likewise, for wear ability and solace, the vast majority of them are more limited long, either over the knee, right on the knee, or somewhat beneath the knee, while conventional kimonos generally are floor length. Furthermore, in conclusion, this sort of dress doesn't need the lot of texture that a customary kimono requires. A customary kimono takes a really broad measure of time to try and put on, while the kimono style dress can for the most part be handily worn and taken off with next to no time and exertion. Its texture is likewise more lightweight and might not have many-sided subtleties.

With the coming of motion pictures like Journals of a Geisha displaying Japanese clothing, numerous western design creators and shoppers of style rushed to the kimono style dress. For sure, the kimono dresses has even been highlighted in Hollywood movies. From enormous mathematical prints to little botanical subtleties, this dress, with its figure complimenting shape makes certain to be a group pleaser among both youthful and old.

THE END

Printed in Great Britain
by Amazon

40615037R00030